MW00881228

READING

J O U R N A L   F O R   K I D S

M I R A B E L L   P U B L I S H I N G

NOTE TO PARENTS

Dear Parent,

Inspiring the love for books from an early age is crucial
to developing a child's literacy skills.

Children grow up so fast. One moment they are solely dependent
on you. Then, in the blink of an eye they are so independent and
throwing tantrums in the supermarket. However, the simple every day
experiences you share with your child will stay with you forever.

This reading journal is a fantastic way to keep track of the books your
child reads. This journal is designed to ensure your child reads at least
one book a week.

This interactive journal is designed to reinforce comprehension
and enhance writing skills. We have provided exploratory tools with
questions to inspire interest and engagement. This journal will help
your child learn how to write book reviews and record their opinions. A
skill that will be useful for future book report assignments as they grow
older.

To help you get started we have provided a list of 25 books for children
(Ages 7-11), most of these books can be borrowed from a local library
or purchased from a bookstore.

Have fun reading!

Mirabell Publishing

25 BOOKS TO READ BEFORE YOU ARE 11 YEARS OLD

1. **The Adventures of Captain Underpants** *by Dav Pilkey*
2. **The Diary of a Killer Cat** *by Anne Fine*
3. **The Guard Dog** *by Dick King-Smith*
4. **How to Train Your Dragon** *by Cressida Cowell*
5. **Little Wolf's Book of Badness** *by Ian Whybrow*
6. **Charlie and the Chocolate Factory** *by Roald Dahl*
7. **The Suitcase Kid** *by Jacqueline Wilson*
8. **The Amazing Story of Adolphus Tips** *by Michael Morpurgo*
9. **Cliffhanger** *by Jacqueline Wilson*
10. **Chitty Chitty Bang Bang Flies Again** *by Frank Cottrell Boyce*
11. **Alice's Adventures in Wonderland** *by Lewis Carroll*
12. **Emily's Legs** *by Dick King-Smith*
13. **Robinson Crusoe** *by Daniel Defoe*
14. **Mr Wolf's Pancakes** *by Jan Fearnley*
15. **Frog is Frog** *by Max Velthuijis*
16. **The Cat Who Lost His Purr** *by Michelle Coxon*
17. **Wizard of Oz** *by Frank Baum*
18. **Jungle Book** *by Rudyard Kipling*
19. **The Lion, the Witch and the Wardrobe** *by C.S. Lewis*
20. **Skulduggery Pleasant** *by Derek Landy*
21. **Charlotte's Web** *by Garth Williams*
22. **Diary of a Wimpy Kid** *by Jeff Kinney*
23. **Meerkat Madness** *by Ian Whybrow*
24. **The Butterfly Lion** *by Michael Morpurgo*
25. **Five on a Treasure Island** *by Enid Blyton*

H A P P Y
READING

DATE <u>22nd of March 2014</u>

BOOK TITLE <u>Little Red Riding Hood</u>

AUTHOR <u>Brothers Grimm</u>

WHAT I LIKED ABOUT THIS BOOK <u>I liked it when the</u>
<u>huntsman put stones in the wolf's tummy and</u>
<u>saved little red riding hood and her grandmother.</u>

I WAS SUPRISED BY <u>How grandma tricked the</u>
<u>second wolf. Also, how much the wolf liked to</u>
<u>eat people.</u>

NEW WORD I LEARNT <u>Huntsman - A huntsman is</u>
<u>someone who hunts wild animals in the forest.</u>

46

HOW TO USE THIS READING JOURNAL

It is important to complete the weekly entries, as it will remind you of your child's favourite book growing up. It will also give a good picture of all the books your child enjoyed reading that year.

Book **20**

MY FAVOURITE CHARACTER *The Huntsman*

THINK OF A NEW TITLE FOR THE BOOK

The Naughty Wolf

WRITE A SHORT LETTER TO THE AUTHOR TELLING HIM OR HER WHAT YOU THOUGHT ABOUT THE BOOK.

Dear Mr Grimm,

I really liked the story. I learnt that it is good to do what my mummy tells me to do.

I am happy the hunstamn saved little red riding hood and her grandma.

Please write more stories for boys and girls.

Thank you

Jessica

THIS BOOK GETS ★ ★ ★ ★ ☆ STARS

DATE _____

BOOK TITLE _____

AUTHOR _____

WHAT I LIKED ABOUT THIS BOOK _____

_____

_____

I WAS SUPRISED BY _____

_____

_____

NEW WORD I LEARNT _____

_____

MY FAVOURITE CHARACTER _____

THINK OF A NEW TITLE FOR THE BOOK

_____

WRITE A SHORT LETTER TO THE AUTHOR TELLING HIM OR HER WHAT
YOU THOUGHT ABOUT THE BOOK.

THIS BOOK GETS ☆ ☆ ☆ ☆ ☆ STARS

DATE _____

BOOK TITLE _____

AUTHOR _____

WHAT I LIKED ABOUT THIS BOOK _____

_____

_____

I WAS SUPRISED BY _____

_____

_____

NEW WORD I LEARNT _____

_____

MY FAVOURITE CHARACTER _____

THINK OF A NEW TITLE FOR THE BOOK

_____

WRITE A SHORT LETTER TO THE AUTHOR TELLING HIM OR HER WHAT
YOU THOUGHT ABOUT THE BOOK.

THIS BOOK GETS ☆ ☆ ☆ ☆ ☆ STARS

DATE

BOOK TITLE

AUTHOR

WHAT I LIKED ABOUT THIS BOOK

I WAS SUPRISED BY

NEW WORD I LEARNT

MY FAVOURITE CHARACTER _____

THINK OF A NEW TITLE FOR THE BOOK

_____

WRITE A SHORT LETTER TO THE AUTHOR TELLING HIM OR HER WHAT YOU THOUGHT ABOUT THE BOOK.

THIS BOOK GETS ☆ ☆ ☆ ☆ ☆ STARS

DATE _____

BOOK TITLE _____

AUTHOR _____

WHAT I LIKED ABOUT THIS BOOK _____

_____

_____

I WAS SUPRISED BY _____

_____

_____

NEW WORD I LEARNT _____

_____

MY FAVOURITE CHARACTER _____

THINK OF A NEW TITLE FOR THE BOOK

_____

WRITE A SHORT LETTER TO THE AUTHOR TELLING HIM OR HER WHAT
YOU THOUGHT ABOUT THE BOOK.

THIS BOOK GETS ☆ ☆ ☆ ☆ ☆ STARS

DATE

BOOK TITLE

AUTHOR

WHAT I LIKED ABOUT THIS BOOK

I WAS SUPRISED BY

NEW WORD I LEARNT

MY FAVOURITE CHARACTER

THINK OF A NEW TITLE FOR THE BOOK

WRITE A SHORT LETTER TO THE AUTHOR TELLING HIM OR HER WHAT YOU THOUGHT ABOUT THE BOOK.

THIS BOOK GETS ☆ ☆ ☆ ☆ ☆ STARS

DATE

BOOK TITLE

AUTHOR

WHAT I LIKED ABOUT THIS BOOK

I WAS SUPRISED BY

NEW WORD I LEARNT

MY FAVOURITE CHARACTER _____

THINK OF A NEW TITLE FOR THE BOOK

_____

WRITE A SHORT LETTER TO THE AUTHOR TELLING HIM OR HER WHAT
YOU THOUGHT ABOUT THE BOOK.

THIS BOOK GETS ☆ ☆ ☆ ☆ ☆ STARS

DATE _____

BOOK TITLE _____

AUTHOR _____

WHAT I LIKED ABOUT THIS BOOK _____

_____

_____

I WAS SUPRISED BY _____

_____

_____

NEW WORD I LEARNT _____

_____

MY FAVOURITE CHARACTER _____

THINK OF A NEW TITLE FOR THE BOOK

_____

WRITE A SHORT LETTER TO THE AUTHOR TELLING HIM OR HER WHAT
YOU THOUGHT ABOUT THE BOOK.

THIS BOOK GETS ☆ ☆ ☆ ☆ ☆ STARS

DATE _____

BOOK TITLE _____

AUTHOR _____

WHAT I LIKED ABOUT THIS BOOK _____

_____

_____

I WAS SUPRISED BY _____

_____

_____

NEW WORD I LEARNT _____

_____

MY FAVOURITE CHARACTER _____

THINK OF A NEW TITLE FOR THE BOOK

_____

WRITE A SHORT LETTER TO THE AUTHOR TELLING HIM OR HER WHAT YOU THOUGHT ABOUT THE BOOK.

THIS BOOK GETS ☆ ☆ ☆ ☆ ☆ STARS

DATE _____

BOOK TITLE _____

AUTHOR _____

WHAT I LIKED ABOUT THIS BOOK _____

_____

_____

I WAS SUPRISED BY _____

_____

_____

NEW WORD I LEARNT _____

_____

MY FAVOURITE CHARACTER _____

THINK OF A NEW TITLE FOR THE BOOK

_____

WRITE A SHORT LETTER TO THE AUTHOR TELLING HIM OR HER WHAT YOU THOUGHT ABOUT THE BOOK.

THIS BOOK GETS ☆ ☆ ☆ ☆ ☆ STARS

DATE _____

BOOK TITLE _____

AUTHOR _____

WHAT I LIKED ABOUT THIS BOOK _____

_____

_____

I WAS SUPRISED BY _____

_____

_____

NEW WORD I LEARNT _____

_____

MY FAVOURITE CHARACTER _____

THINK OF A NEW TITLE FOR THE BOOK

_____

WRITE A SHORT LETTER TO THE AUTHOR TELLING HIM OR HER WHAT
YOU THOUGHT ABOUT THE BOOK.

THIS BOOK GETS ☆ ☆ ☆ ☆ ☆ STARS

DATE _____

BOOK TITLE _____

AUTHOR _____

WHAT I LIKED ABOUT THIS BOOK _____

_____

_____

I WAS SUPRISED BY _____

_____

_____

NEW WORD I LEARNT _____

_____

MY FAVOURITE CHARACTER _____

THINK OF A NEW TITLE FOR THE BOOK

_____

WRITE A SHORT LETTER TO THE AUTHOR TELLING HIM OR HER WHAT
YOU THOUGHT ABOUT THE BOOK.

THIS BOOK GETS ☆ ☆ ☆ ☆ ☆ STARS

DATE _____

BOOK TITLE _____

AUTHOR _____

WHAT I LIKED ABOUT THIS BOOK _____

_____

_____

I WAS SUPRISED BY _____

_____

_____

NEW WORD I LEARNT _____

_____

MY FAVOURITE CHARACTER _____

THINK OF A NEW TITLE FOR THE BOOK

_____

WRITE A SHORT LETTER TO THE AUTHOR TELLING HIM OR HER WHAT
YOU THOUGHT ABOUT THE BOOK.

THIS BOOK GETS ☆ ☆ ☆ ☆ ☆ STARS

DATE _____

BOOK TITLE _____

AUTHOR _____

WHAT I LIKED ABOUT THIS BOOK _____

_____

_____

I WAS SUPRISED BY _____

_____

_____

NEW WORD I LEARNT _____

_____

MY FAVOURITE CHARACTER _____

THINK OF A NEW TITLE FOR THE BOOK

_____

WRITE A SHORT LETTER TO THE AUTHOR TELLING HIM OR HER WHAT YOU THOUGHT ABOUT THE BOOK.

THIS BOOK GETS ☆ ☆ ☆ ☆ ☆ STARS

DATE _____

BOOK TITLE _____

AUTHOR _____

WHAT I LIKED ABOUT THIS BOOK _____

_____

_____

I WAS SUPRISED BY _____

_____

_____

NEW WORD I LEARNT _____

_____

MY FAVOURITE CHARACTER _____

THINK OF A NEW TITLE FOR THE BOOK

_____

WRITE A SHORT LETTER TO THE AUTHOR TELLING HIM OR HER WHAT YOU THOUGHT ABOUT THE BOOK.

THIS BOOK GETS ☆ ☆ ☆ ☆ ☆ STARS

DATE _____

BOOK TITLE _____

AUTHOR _____

WHAT I LIKED ABOUT THIS BOOK _____

_____

_____

I WAS SUPRISED BY _____

_____

_____

NEW WORD I LEARNT _____

_____

MY FAVOURITE CHARACTER _____

THINK OF A NEW TITLE FOR THE BOOK

_____

WRITE A SHORT LETTER TO THE AUTHOR TELLING HIM OR HER WHAT YOU THOUGHT ABOUT THE BOOK.

THIS BOOK GETS ☆ ☆ ☆ ☆ ☆ STARS

DATE _____

BOOK TITLE _____

AUTHOR _____

WHAT I LIKED ABOUT THIS BOOK _____

_____

_____

I WAS SUPRISED BY _____

_____

_____

NEW WORD I LEARNT _____

_____

MY FAVOURITE CHARACTER _____

THINK OF A NEW TITLE FOR THE BOOK

_____

WRITE A SHORT LETTER TO THE AUTHOR TELLING HIM OR HER WHAT
YOU THOUGHT ABOUT THE BOOK.

THIS BOOK GETS ☆ ☆ ☆ ☆ ☆ STARS

DATE _____

BOOK TITLE _____

AUTHOR _____

WHAT I LIKED ABOUT THIS BOOK _____

_____

_____

I WAS SUPRISED BY _____

_____

_____

NEW WORD I LEARNT _____

_____

MY FAVOURITE CHARACTER _____

THINK OF A NEW TITLE FOR THE BOOK

_____

WRITE A SHORT LETTER TO THE AUTHOR TELLING HIM OR HER WHAT YOU THOUGHT ABOUT THE BOOK.

THIS BOOK GETS ☆ ☆ ☆ ☆ ☆ STARS

DATE _____

BOOK TITLE _____

AUTHOR _____

WHAT I LIKED ABOUT THIS BOOK _____

_____

_____

I WAS SUPRISED BY _____

_____

_____

NEW WORD I LEARNT _____

_____

MY FAVOURITE CHARACTER _____

THINK OF A NEW TITLE FOR THE BOOK

_____

WRITE A SHORT LETTER TO THE AUTHOR TELLING HIM OR HER WHAT YOU THOUGHT ABOUT THE BOOK.

THIS BOOK GETS ☆ ☆ ☆ ☆ ☆ STARS

DATE

BOOK TITLE

AUTHOR

WHAT I LIKED ABOUT THIS BOOK

I WAS SUPRISED BY

NEW WORD I LEARNT

MY FAVOURITE CHARACTER _____

THINK OF A NEW TITLE FOR THE BOOK

_____

WRITE A SHORT LETTER TO THE AUTHOR TELLING HIM OR HER WHAT YOU THOUGHT ABOUT THE BOOK.

THIS BOOK GETS ☆ ☆ ☆ ☆ ☆ STARS

DATE _____

BOOK TITLE _____

AUTHOR _____

WHAT I LIKED ABOUT THIS BOOK _____

_____

_____

I WAS SUPRISED BY _____

_____

_____

NEW WORD I LEARNT _____

_____

MY FAVOURITE CHARACTER _____

THINK OF A NEW TITLE FOR THE BOOK

_____

WRITE A SHORT LETTER TO THE AUTHOR TELLING HIM OR HER WHAT YOU THOUGHT ABOUT THE BOOK.

THIS BOOK GETS ☆ ☆ ☆ ☆ ☆ STARS

DATE

BOOK TITLE

AUTHOR

WHAT I LIKED ABOUT THIS BOOK

I WAS SUPRISED BY

NEW WORD I LEARNT

MY FAVOURITE CHARACTER _____

THINK OF A NEW TITLE FOR THE BOOK

_____

WRITE A SHORT LETTER TO THE AUTHOR TELLING HIM OR HER WHAT YOU THOUGHT ABOUT THE BOOK.

THIS BOOK GETS ☆ ☆ ☆ ☆ ☆ STARS

DATE _____

BOOK TITLE _____

AUTHOR _____

WHAT I LIKED ABOUT THIS BOOK _____

_____

_____

I WAS SUPRISED BY _____

_____

_____

NEW WORD I LEARNT _____

_____

MY FAVOURITE CHARACTER _____

THINK OF A NEW TITLE FOR THE BOOK

_____

WRITE A SHORT LETTER TO THE AUTHOR TELLING HIM OR HER WHAT YOU THOUGHT ABOUT THE BOOK.

THIS BOOK GETS ☆ ☆ ☆ ☆ ☆ STARS

DATE _____

BOOK TITLE _____

AUTHOR _____

WHAT I LIKED ABOUT THIS BOOK _____

_____

_____

I WAS SUPRISED BY _____

_____

_____

NEW WORD I LEARNT _____

_____

MY FAVOURITE CHARACTER _____

THINK OF A NEW TITLE FOR THE BOOK

_____

WRITE A SHORT LETTER TO THE AUTHOR TELLING HIM OR HER WHAT YOU THOUGHT ABOUT THE BOOK.

THIS BOOK GETS ☆ ☆ ☆ ☆ ☆ STARS

DATE _____

BOOK TITLE _____

AUTHOR _____

WHAT I LIKED ABOUT THIS BOOK _____

_____

_____

I WAS SUPRISED BY _____

_____

_____

NEW WORD I LEARNT _____

_____

MY FAVOURITE CHARACTER _____

THINK OF A NEW TITLE FOR THE BOOK

_____

WRITE A SHORT LETTER TO THE AUTHOR TELLING HIM OR HER WHAT YOU THOUGHT ABOUT THE BOOK.

THIS BOOK GETS ☆ ☆ ☆ ☆ ☆ STARS

DATE _____

BOOK TITLE _____

AUTHOR _____

WHAT I LIKED ABOUT THIS BOOK _____

_____

_____

I WAS SUPRISED BY _____

_____

_____

NEW WORD I LEARNT _____

_____

MY FAVOURITE CHARACTER _____

THINK OF A NEW TITLE FOR THE BOOK

_____

WRITE A SHORT LETTER TO THE AUTHOR TELLING HIM OR HER WHAT YOU THOUGHT ABOUT THE BOOK.

THIS BOOK GETS ☆ ☆ ☆ ☆ ☆ STARS

DATE

BOOK TITLE

AUTHOR

WHAT I LIKED ABOUT THIS BOOK

I WAS SUPRISED BY

NEW WORD I LEARNT

MY FAVOURITE CHARACTER _____

THINK OF A NEW TITLE FOR THE BOOK

_____

WRITE A SHORT LETTER TO THE AUTHOR TELLING HIM OR HER WHAT
YOU THOUGHT ABOUT THE BOOK.

THIS BOOK GETS ☆ ☆ ☆ ☆ ☆ STARS

DATE _____

BOOK TITLE _____

AUTHOR _____

WHAT I LIKED ABOUT THIS BOOK _____

_____

_____

I WAS SUPRISED BY _____

_____

_____

NEW WORD I LEARNT _____

_____

MY FAVOURITE CHARACTER

THINK OF A NEW TITLE FOR THE BOOK

WRITE A SHORT LETTER TO THE AUTHOR TELLING HIM OR HER WHAT YOU THOUGHT ABOUT THE BOOK.

THIS BOOK GETS ☆ ☆ ☆ ☆ ☆ STARS

DATE _____

BOOK TITLE _____

AUTHOR _____

WHAT I LIKED ABOUT THIS BOOK _____

_____

_____

I WAS SUPRISED BY _____

_____

_____

NEW WORD I LEARNT _____

_____

MY FAVOURITE CHARACTER _____

THINK OF A NEW TITLE FOR THE BOOK

_____

WRITE A SHORT LETTER TO THE AUTHOR TELLING HIM OR HER WHAT YOU THOUGHT ABOUT THE BOOK.

THIS BOOK GETS ☆ ☆ ☆ ☆ ☆ STARS

DATE

BOOK TITLE

AUTHOR

WHAT I LIKED ABOUT THIS BOOK

I WAS SUPRISED BY

NEW WORD I LEARNT

MY FAVOURITE CHARACTER _____

THINK OF A NEW TITLE FOR THE BOOK

_____

WRITE A SHORT LETTER TO THE AUTHOR TELLING HIM OR HER WHAT YOU THOUGHT ABOUT THE BOOK.

THIS BOOK GETS ☆ ☆ ☆ ☆ ☆ STARS

DATE _____

BOOK TITLE _____

AUTHOR _____

WHAT I LIKED ABOUT THIS BOOK _____

_____

_____

I WAS SUPRISED BY _____

_____

_____

NEW WORD I LEARNT _____

_____

MY FAVOURITE CHARACTER _____

THINK OF A NEW TITLE FOR THE BOOK

_____

WRITE A SHORT LETTER TO THE AUTHOR TELLING HIM OR HER WHAT YOU THOUGHT ABOUT THE BOOK.

THIS BOOK GETS ☆ ☆ ☆ ☆ ☆ STARS

DATE _____

BOOK TITLE _____

AUTHOR _____

WHAT I LIKED ABOUT THIS BOOK _____

_____

_____

I WAS SUPRISED BY _____

_____

_____

NEW WORD I LEARNT _____

_____

MY FAVOURITE CHARACTER _____

THINK OF A NEW TITLE FOR THE BOOK

_____

WRITE A SHORT LETTER TO THE AUTHOR TELLING HIM OR HER WHAT
YOU THOUGHT ABOUT THE BOOK.

THIS BOOK GETS ☆ ☆ ☆ ☆ ☆ STARS

DATE _____

BOOK TITLE _____

AUTHOR _____

WHAT I LIKED ABOUT THIS BOOK _____

_____

_____

I WAS SUPRISED BY _____

_____

_____

NEW WORD I LEARNT _____

_____

MY FAVOURITE CHARACTER _____

THINK OF A NEW TITLE FOR THE BOOK

_____

WRITE A SHORT LETTER TO THE AUTHOR TELLING HIM OR HER WHAT
YOU THOUGHT ABOUT THE BOOK.

THIS BOOK GETS ☆ ☆ ☆ ☆ ☆ STARS

DATE _____

BOOK TITLE _____

AUTHOR _____

WHAT I LIKED ABOUT THIS BOOK _____

_____

_____

I WAS SUPRISED BY _____

_____

_____

NEW WORD I LEARNT _____

_____

MY FAVOURITE CHARACTER _____

THINK OF A NEW TITLE FOR THE BOOK

_____

WRITE A SHORT LETTER TO THE AUTHOR TELLING HIM OR HER WHAT
YOU THOUGHT ABOUT THE BOOK.

THIS BOOK GETS ☆ ☆ ☆ ☆ ☆ STARS

DATE

BOOK TITLE

AUTHOR

WHAT I LIKED ABOUT THIS BOOK

I WAS SUPRISED BY

NEW WORD I LEARNT

MY FAVOURITE CHARACTER _____

THINK OF A NEW TITLE FOR THE BOOK

_____

WRITE A SHORT LETTER TO THE AUTHOR TELLING HIM OR HER WHAT
YOU THOUGHT ABOUT THE BOOK.

THIS BOOK GETS ☆ ☆ ☆ ☆ ☆ STARS

DATE _____

BOOK TITLE _____

AUTHOR _____

WHAT I LIKED ABOUT THIS BOOK _____

_____

_____

I WAS SUPRISED BY _____

_____

_____

NEW WORD I LEARNT _____

_____

MY FAVOURITE CHARACTER   _____

THINK OF A NEW TITLE FOR THE BOOK

_____

WRITE A SHORT LETTER TO THE AUTHOR TELLING HIM OR HER WHAT YOU THOUGHT ABOUT THE BOOK.

THIS BOOK GETS ☆ ☆ ☆ ☆ ☆ STARS

DATE _____

BOOK TITLE _____

AUTHOR _____

WHAT I LIKED ABOUT THIS BOOK _____

_____

_____

I WAS SUPRISED BY _____

_____

_____

NEW WORD I LEARNT _____

_____

MY FAVOURITE CHARACTER   _____

THINK OF A NEW TITLE FOR THE BOOK

_____

WRITE A SHORT LETTER TO THE AUTHOR TELLING HIM OR HER WHAT YOU THOUGHT ABOUT THE BOOK.

THIS BOOK GETS ☆ ☆ ☆ ☆ ☆ STARS

DATE

BOOK TITLE

AUTHOR

WHAT I LIKED ABOUT THIS BOOK

I WAS SUPRISED BY

NEW WORD I LEARNT

MY FAVOURITE CHARACTER _____

THINK OF A NEW TITLE FOR THE BOOK

_____

WRITE A SHORT LETTER TO THE AUTHOR TELLING HIM OR HER WHAT YOU THOUGHT ABOUT THE BOOK.

THIS BOOK GETS ☆ ☆ ☆ ☆ ☆ STARS

DATE _____

BOOK TITLE _____

AUTHOR _____

WHAT I LIKED ABOUT THIS BOOK _____

_____

_____

I WAS SUPRISED BY _____

_____

_____

NEW WORD I LEARNT _____

_____

MY FAVOURITE CHARACTER _____

THINK OF A NEW TITLE FOR THE BOOK

_____

WRITE A SHORT LETTER TO THE AUTHOR TELLING HIM OR HER WHAT YOU THOUGHT ABOUT THE BOOK.

THIS BOOK GETS ☆ ☆ ☆ ☆ ☆ STARS

DATE _____

BOOK TITLE _____

AUTHOR _____

WHAT I LIKED ABOUT THIS BOOK _____

_____

_____

I WAS SUPRISED BY _____

_____

_____

NEW WORD I LEARNT _____

_____

MY FAVOURITE CHARACTER _____

THINK OF A NEW TITLE FOR THE BOOK

_____

WRITE A SHORT LETTER TO THE AUTHOR TELLING HIM OR HER WHAT
YOU THOUGHT ABOUT THE BOOK.

THIS BOOK GETS ☆ ☆ ☆ ☆ ☆ STARS

DATE _____

BOOK TITLE _____

AUTHOR _____

WHAT I LIKED ABOUT THIS BOOK _____

_____

_____

I WAS SUPRISED BY _____

_____

_____

NEW WORD I LEARNT _____

_____

MY FAVOURITE CHARACTER _____

THINK OF A NEW TITLE FOR THE BOOK

_____

WRITE A SHORT LETTER TO THE AUTHOR TELLING HIM OR HER WHAT
YOU THOUGHT ABOUT THE BOOK.

THIS BOOK GETS ☆ ☆ ☆ ☆ ☆ STARS

DATE _____

BOOK TITLE _____

AUTHOR _____

WHAT I LIKED ABOUT THIS BOOK _____

_____

_____

I WAS SUPRISED BY _____

_____

_____

NEW WORD I LEARNT _____

_____

MY FAVOURITE CHARACTER _____

THINK OF A NEW TITLE FOR THE BOOK

_____

WRITE A SHORT LETTER TO THE AUTHOR TELLING HIM OR HER WHAT
YOU THOUGHT ABOUT THE BOOK.

THIS BOOK GETS ☆ ☆ ☆ ☆ ☆ STARS

DATE _____

BOOK TITLE _____

AUTHOR _____

WHAT I LIKED ABOUT THIS BOOK _____

_____

_____

I WAS SUPRISED BY _____

_____

_____

NEW WORD I LEARNT _____

_____

MY FAVOURITE CHARACTER _____

THINK OF A NEW TITLE FOR THE BOOK

_____

WRITE A SHORT LETTER TO THE AUTHOR TELLING HIM OR HER WHAT YOU THOUGHT ABOUT THE BOOK.

THIS BOOK GETS ☆ ☆ ☆ ☆ ☆ STARS

DATE _____

BOOK TITLE _____

AUTHOR _____

WHAT I LIKED ABOUT THIS BOOK _____

_____

_____

I WAS SUPRISED BY _____

_____

_____

NEW WORD I LEARNT _____

_____

MY FAVOURITE CHARACTER _____

THINK OF A NEW TITLE FOR THE BOOK

_____

WRITE A SHORT LETTER TO THE AUTHOR TELLING HIM OR HER WHAT YOU THOUGHT ABOUT THE BOOK.

THIS BOOK GETS ☆ ☆ ☆ ☆ ☆ STARS

DATE _____

BOOK TITLE _____

AUTHOR _____

WHAT I LIKED ABOUT THIS BOOK _____

_____

_____

I WAS SUPRISED BY _____

_____

_____

NEW WORD I LEARNT _____

_____

MY FAVOURITE CHARACTER _____

THINK OF A NEW TITLE FOR THE BOOK

_____

WRITE A SHORT LETTER TO THE AUTHOR TELLING HIM OR HER WHAT YOU THOUGHT ABOUT THE BOOK.

THIS BOOK GETS ☆ ☆ ☆ ☆ ☆ STARS

DATE _____

BOOK TITLE _____

AUTHOR _____

WHAT I LIKED ABOUT THIS BOOK _____

_____

_____

I WAS SUPRISED BY _____

_____

_____

NEW WORD I LEARNT _____

_____

MY FAVOURITE CHARACTER _____

THINK OF A NEW TITLE FOR THE BOOK

_____

WRITE A SHORT LETTER TO THE AUTHOR TELLING HIM OR HER WHAT
YOU THOUGHT ABOUT THE BOOK.

THIS BOOK GETS ☆ ☆ ☆ ☆ ☆ STARS

DATE _____

BOOK TITLE _____

AUTHOR _____

WHAT I LIKED ABOUT THIS BOOK _____

_____

_____

I WAS SUPRISED BY _____

_____

_____

NEW WORD I LEARNT _____

_____

MY FAVOURITE CHARACTER _____

THINK OF A NEW TITLE FOR THE BOOK

_____

WRITE A SHORT LETTER TO THE AUTHOR TELLING HIM OR HER WHAT YOU THOUGHT ABOUT THE BOOK.

THIS BOOK GETS ☆ ☆ ☆ ☆ ☆ STARS

DATE _____

BOOK TITLE _____

AUTHOR _____

WHAT I LIKED ABOUT THIS BOOK _____

_____

_____

I WAS SUPRISED BY _____

_____

_____

NEW WORD I LEARNT _____

_____

MY FAVOURITE CHARACTER _____

THINK OF A NEW TITLE FOR THE BOOK

_____

WRITE A SHORT LETTER TO THE AUTHOR TELLING HIM OR HER WHAT
YOU THOUGHT ABOUT THE BOOK.

THIS BOOK GETS ☆ ☆ ☆ ☆ ☆ STARS

DATE

BOOK TITLE

AUTHOR

WHAT I LIKED ABOUT THIS BOOK

I WAS SUPRISED BY

NEW WORD I LEARNT

MY FAVOURITE CHARACTER _____

THINK OF A NEW TITLE FOR THE BOOK

_____

WRITE A SHORT LETTER TO THE AUTHOR TELLING HIM OR HER WHAT YOU THOUGHT ABOUT THE BOOK.

THIS BOOK GETS ☆ ☆ ☆ ☆ ☆ STARS

DATE _____

BOOK TITLE _____

AUTHOR _____

WHAT I LIKED ABOUT THIS BOOK _____

_____

_____

I WAS SUPRISED BY _____

_____

_____

NEW WORD I LEARNT _____

_____

MY FAVOURITE CHARACTER   _____

THINK OF A NEW TITLE FOR THE BOOK

_____

WRITE A SHORT LETTER TO THE AUTHOR TELLING HIM OR HER WHAT YOU THOUGHT ABOUT THE BOOK.

THIS BOOK GETS ☆ ☆ ☆ ☆ ☆ STARS

DATE _____

BOOK TITLE _____

AUTHOR _____

WHAT I LIKED ABOUT THIS BOOK _____

_____

_____

I WAS SUPRISED BY _____

_____

_____

NEW WORD I LEARNT _____

_____

MY FAVOURITE CHARACTER _____

THINK OF A NEW TITLE FOR THE BOOK

_____

WRITE A SHORT LETTER TO THE AUTHOR TELLING HIM OR HER WHAT
YOU THOUGHT ABOUT THE BOOK.

THIS BOOK GETS ☆ ☆ ☆ ☆ ☆ STARS

DATE _____

BOOK TITLE _____

AUTHOR _____

WHAT I LIKED ABOUT THIS BOOK _____

_____

_____

I WAS SUPRISED BY _____

_____

_____

NEW WORD I LEARNT _____

_____

MY FAVOURITE CHARACTER _____

THINK OF A NEW TITLE FOR THE BOOK

_____

WRITE A SHORT LETTER TO THE AUTHOR TELLING HIM OR HER WHAT
YOU THOUGHT ABOUT THE BOOK.

THIS BOOK GETS ☆ ☆ ☆ ☆ ☆ STARS

DATE

BOOK TITLE

AUTHOR

WHAT I LIKED ABOUT THIS BOOK

I WAS SUPRISED BY

NEW WORD I LEARNT

MY FAVOURITE CHARACTER _____

THINK OF A NEW TITLE FOR THE BOOK

_____

WRITE A SHORT LETTER TO THE AUTHOR TELLING HIM OR HER WHAT YOU THOUGHT ABOUT THE BOOK.

THIS BOOK GETS ☆ ☆ ☆ ☆ ☆ STARS

OTHER JOURNALS FROM
MIRABELL PUBLISHING

We have the following Journals for kids, which are all available on Amazon:

GRATITUDE JOURNALS

- Gratitude Journal for Kids: My Gratitude Journal
- Gratitude Journal for Kids: 30 Days of Gratitude
- Gratitude Journal for Kids: 52 Weeks of Gratitude
- Gratitude Journal for Kids: 365 Days of Gratitude

TRAVEL JOURNALS

5 - 9 years
- My Travel Journal: A Journal for 5 Family Vacations
- My Travel Journal: A Journal for 10 Family Vacations

10 - 15 years
- My Travel Journal: A Journal for 5 Family Vacations
- My Travel Journal: A Journal for 10 Family Vacations

Made in the USA
Monee, IL
26 August 2020